Circle of Life
Pond Life

Written by David Stewart
Illustrated by Carolyn Scrace
Created and designed by David Salariya

W
FRANKLIN WATTS
LONDON•SYDNEY

Contents

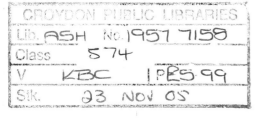

Introduction

Every pond is different. Many of the plants, insects and animals shown in this book may be found in ponds near you.

Frogs, newts, fish and some birds all live on or in ponds. In this book, you will see how they find mates, how their young are born and how the young grow into adults.

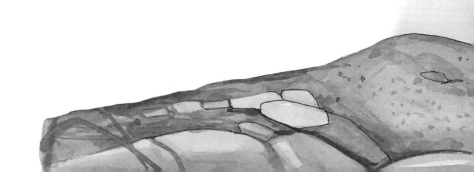

Fox

Magpie

Male frog

Finding a mate

In the spring all the creatures living in and around the pond begin to look for mates.

The male frog sits on a lily pad in the sun. Frogs spend most of their lives in or close to fresh water.

Male stickleback

Newt

Great pond snail

8

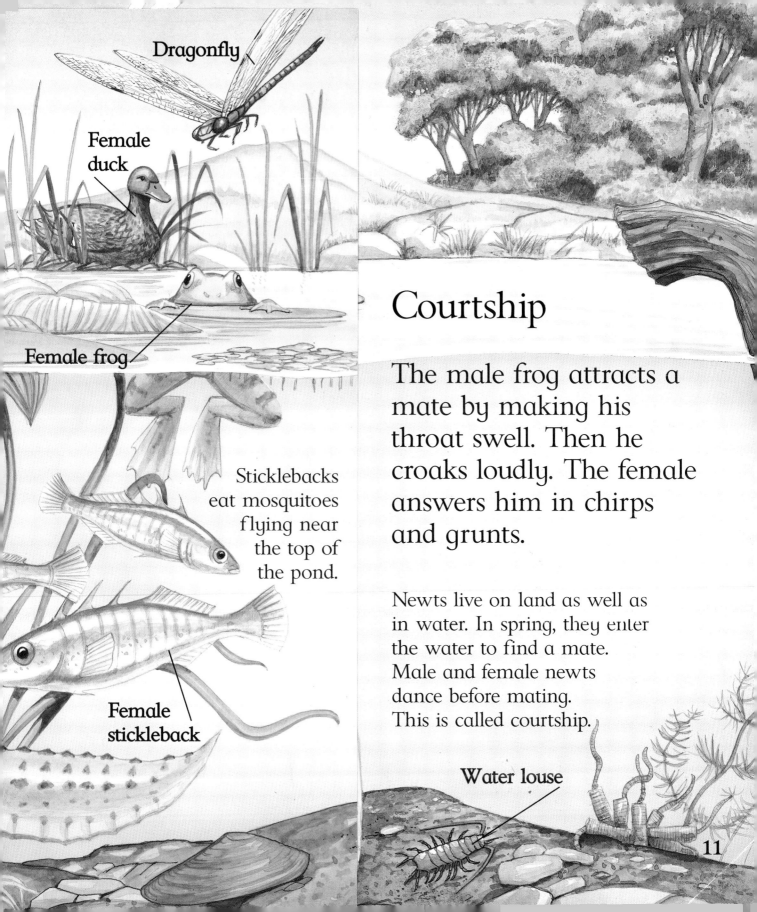

Dragonfly

Female duck

Female frog

Sticklebacks eat mosquitoes flying near the top of the pond.

Female stickleback

Courtship

The male frog attracts a mate by making his throat swell. Then he croaks loudly. The female answers him in chirps and grunts.

Newts live on land as well as in water. In spring, they enter the water to find a mate. Male and female newts dance before mating. This is called courtship.

Water louse

11

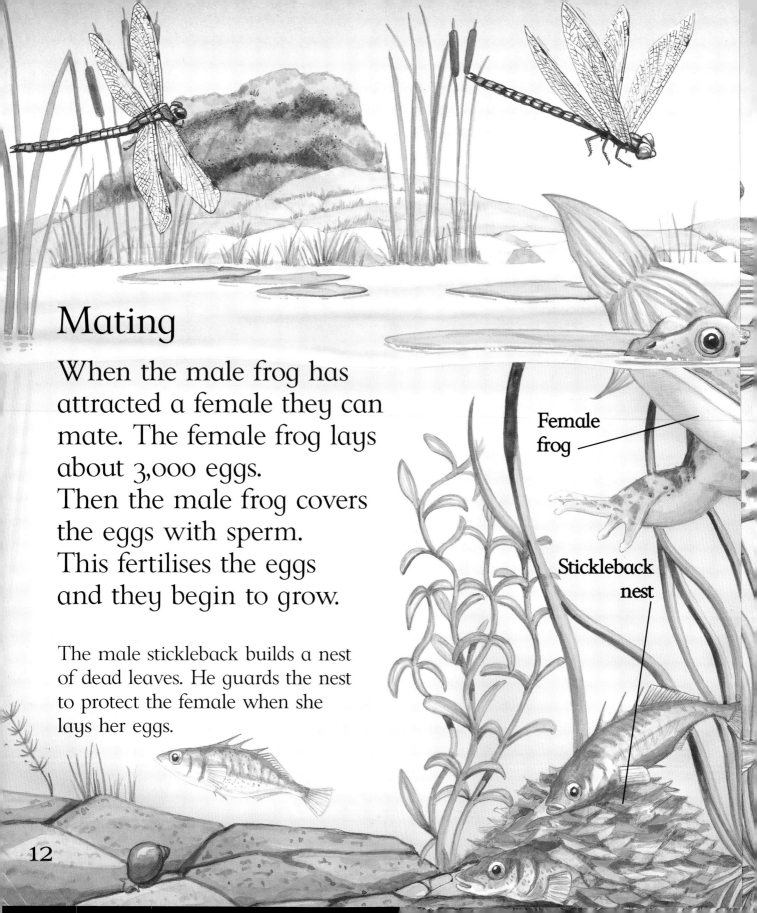

Mating

When the male frog has attracted a female they can mate. The female frog lays about 3,000 eggs. Then the male frog covers the eggs with sperm. This fertilises the eggs and they begin to grow.

The male stickleback builds a nest of dead leaves. He guards the nest to protect the female when she lays her eggs.

Female frog

Stickleback nest

Kingfisher

The eggs hatch

The fertilised frog's eggs stick together and sink to the bottom of the pond.

Male frog

Saucer bug

The jelly around the eggs swells and forms frogspawn. A few days later tadpoles hatch from the eggs.

Pond worm

13

15

Tadpoles

Seven weeks after hatching, the tadpoles still live underwater. They breathe through their gills and eat tiny plants.

The tadpoles' back legs start to grow. As they get bigger, tadpoles eat small water animals like water fleas and pond worms.

Water spider's air bubble

Pond worm

Duckling

Dangerous times

Two weeks later, the tadpoles' gills disappear. The tadpoles then start to breathe using lungs.

Many creatures in the pond like to eat tadpoles. Even insects such as the great diving beetle will catch and eat them.

Young newt

Water flea

Gills

Tadpole

Water scorpion

17

19

Caddis fly

Pond skater

From tadpoles to froglets

As spring turns into summer the tadpoles become young frogs, called froglets. They can now swim to the surface of the pond and breathe air. Froglets have long sticky tongues, good for catching insects.

From froglets to frogs

Frogs are amphibians. This means they can live in and out of water. Above the surface of the pond, the fully grown frogs can be a good meal for a fox.

Pike are a danger to every small creature in the pond. They lie close to plants and catch their prey by surprise.

Froglets

Autumn arrives

All the animals born in
the spring are now adults.
As summer changes to
autumn the weather
becomes cooler and wetter.
Birds migrate to warmer
places. Some animals
prepare to hibernate.

Caddis fly
larva case

Winter settles in

Carp

Life in the pond is much quieter in winter. Many creatures and plants look dead, but they are not. They are saving their energy for when the warmer weather returns in the spring.

Fallen leaves sink to the bottom of the pond and start to rot.

The frog has found a place to hibernate. He will sleep all through winter among the rotting leaves at the bottom of the pond.

25

27

Pond life through the year

In spring, the adult frogs look for mates.

Many of the pond animals go through courtship dances to attract a mate.

During mating, the female frog's eggs are fertilised by the male.

After 21 days tadpoles hatch from the frogspawn.

The tadpoles grow into froglets. Their gills disappear and the froglets breathe with lungs.

By the end of the summer, the froglets have become fully grown frogs. They will soon be looking for their own mates.

29

Words about pond life

Amphibians
Creatures able to live in water or on land. They begin their lives in water.

Courtship
The special things a male does to attract a female.

Fertilisation
When an egg and sperm join together. The egg and sperm will become a baby.

Froglet
A young frog.

Frogspawn
The sticky eggs of a frog that float on the surface of the water. Tadpoles hatch from frogspawn.

Gills
These are needed by animals to breathe underwater. They are on the outside of the body.

Hatch
When a baby creature comes out of its egg.

Hibernate
To sleep through the winter.

Larva
The form an insect takes after hatching from its egg.

Lungs
These are needed by creatures to breathe air. They are inside the body.

Mating
The joining of a male (father) to a female (mother) to make babies.

Migrate
When an animal travels a long way, at certain times of the year, to find a warmer or cooler place to live.

Nymph
A young dragonfly.

Prey
An animal that is killed by another for food.

Sperm
The liquid from the male that joins the egg from the female to produce a baby.

Tadpole
The small creature that hatches from a frog's egg.

Index

Language Consultant: Betty Root
Natural History Consultant: Dr Gerald Legg

Editors: Karen Barker Smith
Stephanie Cole

© The Salariya Book Company Ltd MMII

Created, designed and produced by
The Salariya Book Company Ltd
Book House,
25 Marlborough Place,
Brighton BN1 1UB

Visit the Salariya Book Company at
www.salariya.com

A CIP catalogue record for this book is available from the British Library.

ISBN 0 7496 4426 5

This edition first published in 2005 by
Franklin Watts
96 Leonard Street,
London EC2A 4XD

Franklin Watts Australia
45-51 Huntley Street,
Alexandria, NSW 2015

Printed in Hong Kong